About the Author

Mrs. Susan Thomas has 8 years of experience in QTP. She has developed automation frameworks using QTP for large software testing projects. She is strong in VBScript and VBA.

She has worked on projects in below domains.

1. Investment Banking
2. Healthcare
3. Logistics
4. Mortgage Banking
5. Retail Banking

Her hobbies are travelling to new tourist places, watching football, cricket and learning latest technological stuff.

Preface

This book covers all topics on VBScript and QTP. QTP is the most popular automation testing tool in the market today. VBScript is used a scripting language in QTP. So you must know how to apply VBScript concepts in QTP.

Major topics covered in this book are.

1. Introduction to VBScript
2. Variables, data types, Arrays
3. Control statements
4. String Handling in QTP
5. Maths functions
6. Date and time functions in QTP
7. Dictionary objects
8. File handling in QTP
9. Error handling in QTP
10. Procedures and functions
11. Classes
12. Regular expressions in Object Repository
13. WSH in QTP
14. WMI in QTP

1. VBScript Basics

In this chapter, You will get to know about VBScript applications and also learn about how to write and execute the simple VBScript program in Windows Operating System.

1.1 VBScript Intoduction

Vbscript is a scripting language used for performing administrative tasks in system programming.

Vb script is a loosely typed language meaning we don't need to define the data type of the variables in vbscript.

It is used only on Microsoft operating system.

1.2 VBScript Applications

VbScript is used in many places.

1. In windows administrative tasks.
2. In QTP as automation testing scripting language.
3. In html pages as a client side scripting language.
4. It is also used in embedded applications
5. VBScript is also used as server side scripting language in native ASP pages with IIS Web Server.

1.3 How to execute VBScript

You can write and execute the vbscript programs on only Windows based machines. You can create the file with extension .vbs and then double click it to execute the code inside it. Below figures show how to do it on windows 7 machine.

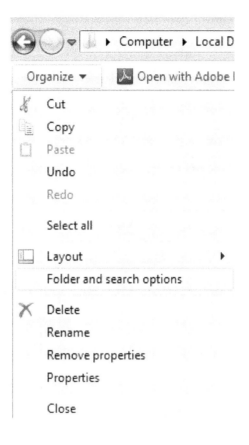

Open Folder and Search Options

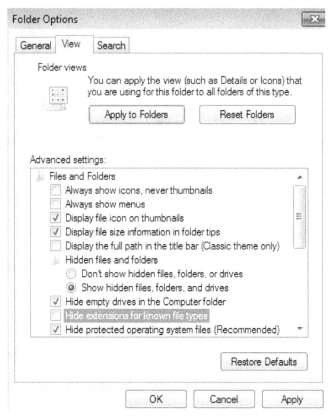

Uncheck hide extensions for known file types

abc.vbs code is given below.

```
Msgbox "first vbscript program"
```

Name

abc.vbs

first program in vbscript

OK

Create a vbscript program in notepad and Save with .vbs extension..
Double click to Execute

To run the same VBScript program in QTP, you need to just copy and paste the code into QTP expert view and run it.

To run any script in this book in QTP, you do not need to make any change. Just copy the code in QTP code Window and Run it.

2. Variables, Data Types and Operators

In this chapter you will learn about variables, data types and operators in VBScript. You will also learn how to change the data type of the variables and find the data type of the variable.

2.1 Variables in Vbscript

Variables are storage locations in memory where we can store the values.

In vb script there are 3 types of variables.

- Scalar - contains only one value.
- Array - contains many values.
- Const - Constant variables.

Scalar variable Example in vb script -

```
Dim a
a = 10
```

In above vb script example we have a variable called a with value as 10. We can store only one value in that variable at any point of time.

Array variable Example in vb script -

```
Dim a (10)
a(1) = 22
a(4) = 23
```

In above vb script example we have a variable called a with size of 10. We can store 11 values in that variable at any point of time.

Const variable Example in vb script -
Const variable is a variable whose value does not change during the execution of the program.

```
const a=10
```

2.2 Data Types in vbscript

In vb script all variables are initialized with the data type called **variant**.

But we can have below sub data types in vb script.

In below table we have mentioned all sub data types in vb script. In next post we will see how to use these sub data types in vb script examples.

Subtype	Description
Empty	**Variable** is uninitialized. Value is 0 or ""
Null	**Variable has** Invalid data.
Boolean	True/False
Byte	Contains integer (0 to 255).

Integer	Contains integer (-32,768 to 32,767).
Currency	-922,337,203,685,477.5808 to 922,337,203,685,477.5807.
Long	Contains integer (-2,147,483,648 to 2,147,483,647).
Single	Contains a single-precision, floating-point number
Double	Contains a double-precision, floating-point number
Date (Time)	Contains a date
String	Contains a String
Object	Contains an object.
Error	Contains an error number.

Examples -

In below example we have a variable x and we have assigned a value 10 to x. In the next statement

when we use typename method to check the data type of variable x then it will show it as a integer.

```
x = 10
```

MsgBox TypeName(x) 'prints integer

```
x = 11.1
```

MsgBox TypeName(x) 'prints double

If we store the value 11.1 in the same variable x, then it's data type will be shown as Double. So this is how data type of the variables keep changing in the VBScript. So VBScript language is called as loosely typed language. And the mechanism to determine the data type of variables at runtime is called as late binding.

Data Type Conversion

We can also convert the data type of the variable explicitly using various data type conversion functions.

For example - In below code we have a VBScript which will convert the decimal number into integer.

```
a = 11.3
```

Msgbox TypeName(a) 'prints double

```
a = cint(a)
```

Msgbox Typename(a) 'prints Integer

Other data type conversion functions are.

1. cdbl - converts to double
2. cstr - converts to string
3. cbool - converts to boolean
4. cbyte - converts to byte
5. ccur - converts to currency
6. cdate - converts to date
7. clng - converts to long integer

2.3 Operators in VBScript

What are the different operators in vbscript?

At broad level there are 3 kinds of operators as mentioned below.

1. Arithmetic Operators
2. Comparison Operators
3. Logical Operators

Arithmetic Operators in the order of precedence and their usage.

- Exponentiation ^
- Unary negation –
- Multiplication *
- Floating point Division /
- Integer division \
- Modulus arithmetic Mod -gets the remainder
- Addition +
- Subtraction –
- String concatenation & - concatenates 2 strings

Comparison Operators and their usage.

- Equality =

- Inequality <>
- Less than <
- Greater than >
- Less than or equal to <=
- Greater than or equal to >=
- Object equivalence Is

Logical Operators in the order of precedence and their usage.

- Logical negation Not
- Logical conjunction And
- Logical disjunction Or
- Logical exclusion Xor
- Logical equivalence Eqv
- Logical implication Imp

Example -

```
if a>10 and b<99 then
    msgbox "a is greater than 10 and b
is less than 99"
end if

msgbox "Remainder after dividing 10 by 3
is -> " & (10 mod 3)
```

2.4 Basic Syntax in VBScript

Remember below points about VBScript Syntax.

1. VBScript is loosely typed language that means you do not need to declare the variables with data type

2. VBScript comments start with symbol '. You can also comment using rem keyword.

3. You do not need to put semicolon at the end of the statement like C,C++ and JAVA

VBScript also provides below functions that can be used to find out more information about the variables.

1. **IsArray** - This function can be used to check if the given variable is an array or not

2. **IsDate** - This function can be used to check if the given variable is a valid date or not

3. **IsEmpty** - This function can be used to check if the given variable is empty or not

4. **IsNull** - This function can be used to check if the given variable is a null or not

5. **IsNumeric** - This function can be used to check if the given variable is valid number or not

6. **IsObject** - This function can be used to check if the given variable is valid object or not

7. **TypeName** - This function returns the data type of the given variable.

Examples -

```vbscript
dim a(4)
dim b
b=10

Msgbox  "a is array? -> " & IsArray(a)
'prints true
```

```
Msgbox   "b is a date? -> " & IsDate(a)
'prints false

Msgbox   "b is empty? -> " & IsEmpty(b)
'prints false

Msgbox   "b is null? -> " & IsNull(b)
'prints false

Msgbox   "b is numeric? -> " &
IsNumeric(b)    'prints true

Msgbox   "b is object? -> " & IsObject(b)
'prints false

Msgbox   "TypeName of b -> " &
TypeName(b)    'prints integer
```

3. Control Statements

In this chapter, you will learn about various control statements in VBScript like if..else, Select...Case, For loop, For each loop, Do ..while loop.

3.1 Conditional Statements

What are different conditional statements in vbscript?

In Vbscript there are 2 types of conditional statements.

1. if ...else
2. Select Case

Example of if else -

```
a = 10

If a > 10 Then
   Msgbox "a is greater than 10"
ElseIf a>0 then
   Msgbox "a is between 0 and 11"
Else
   Msgbox "a is not greater than 0"
End If
```

Select Case Flow Chart

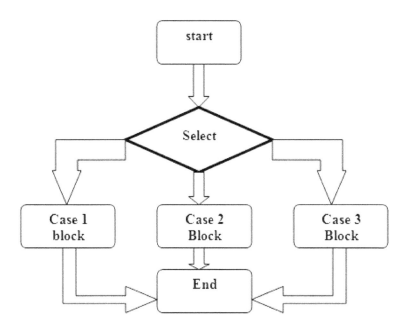

Figure 1 - Select Case Flow Chart

Example of select case -

```
a = Inputbox("enter the number")

Select Case cint(a)

  Case 1

    msgbox "You entered 1"

  Case 2
    msgbox "You entered 2"

  Case 3
    msgbox "You entered 3"
```

```
Case else
    msgbox "You entered invalid input"

End Select
```

3.2 Looping Statements

Here is the list of different looping statements in vbscript.

1. For ....Next
2. For Each ...Next
3. Do While...Loop
4. Do Until....Loop
5. While...Wend

You can exit from For Loop with Exit For statement

1) For Loop

As shown in below flowchart, we can repeat the code using for loop till the condition is true.

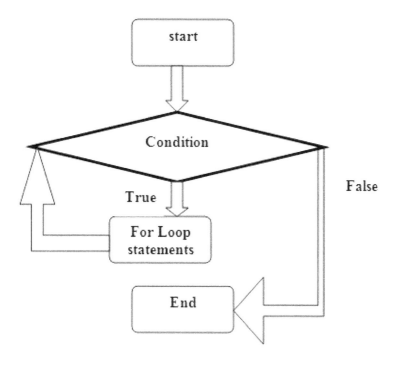

Figure 2 - For loop

```
For i=1 to 3
    Msgbox i*i
Next

'For Each loop
a  = array(22,33,5,3)
For each e in a
    Msgbox a
Next
```

You can exit from Do Loop with Exit Do statement

2) do while ...loop

```
i=1
Do while (i<3)
 Msgbox i*i
  i=i+1
Loop
```

3) do until ....loop

```
i=1
Do until i>3
 Msgbox i*i
  i=i+1
Loop
```

You can not exit from while loop using exit statement.

4) while........wend

```
i=1
While i<=3
 Msgbox i*i
  i=i+1
Wend
```

4. Arrays in VBScript

In this chapter, you will learn about Arrays in VBScript. You will learn how to declare static and dynamic arrays in VBScript. You will also learn how to access elements in the array and different operations on the array like filter, sort, join etc.

4.1 Declaring arrays in vb script

Arrays are used to store multiple values in the same variable. In any QTP test, arrays are definitely used. Some of the scenarios where we will use arrays in QTP are given below.

1. Store the parameters passed from the Test Data Sheet.
2. Store the values from the application for later use.

   We can define array in vb script in 4 different ways.

- dim a(10) - static array of 11 elements
- dim b()   - dynamic array
- a = array(1,2,3,4) - declare array with values
- a = split("as*dfdf*sdsd","*") - array is automatically created with a(0) = as, a(1)=dfdf , a(2)=sdsd

Various Operations that can be performed on the array are mentioned below

1. Iterate through all elements in the array

2. Find the lower bound and upper bound of the array
3. Filter the array
4. Join the elements in the array
5. Sort the elements in the array

1. Iterate through all elements in the array

Below example will illustrate how we can access all elements in the array.

```
a = array(34,5,66,"sagar", 44.4)

for i=0 to ubound(a)

    'Print each element in the array one
by one.
    msgbox a(i)

next
```

2.Find the upper bound and lower bound in the array

Below example will illustrate how we can find the upper bound and lower bound of the array.

```
a = array(34,5,66,"sagar", 44.4)
Msgbox ubound(a) 'print 4
Msgbox lbound(a) 'prints 0
```

3.Filter the array

We can use filter function to filter elements in the array.

Syntax of the Filter method is given below.
'Filter(arrayToSearch,substringToSearch[,include [,compare]])

1. arrayToSearch - This is the array whose elements will be searched
2. substringToSearch - String to search in array
3. include - this can be true/false. If true, it will return all matching values If false, it will return all non-matching values. Default is true.
4. compare - this flag can be 0 or 1. If 0 means it will be binary comparison. else it will be textual comparison. Default is binary comparison -0

Below example will illustrate how we can filter the elements in array.

```
a = array("amol","sachin","arjun","Sagar")
b = filter(a,"s",true,0)
' b = filter(a,"s")    .....both are
same ...binary comparison....case
sensitive

for i=0 to ubound(b)

    msgbox b(i)   'will print sachin

next

'****************************************************
```

```
a =
array("amol","sachin","arjun","Sagar")
b = filter(a,"s",true,1)

for i=0 to ubound(b)

  msgbox b(i)      'will print sachin and
Sagar........textual comparison....case
insensitive

next

'************************************************************

a =
array("amol","sachin","arjun","Sagar")
b = filter(a,"s",false,1)

for i=0 to ubound(b)

   msgbox b(i)      'will print amol and
arjun ........non-matching elements.

Next
```

4. Join the elements in the array

Join function is used to join the elements in the array.

```
a = array("sachin", "plays", "cricket")
msgbox join(a)   'will print sachin plays
cricket
a = array("sachin", "plays", "cricket")
msgbox join(a,"*")   'will print
sachin*plays*cricket
```

4.2 Types of Array in vb script

There are 2 types of arrays in vb script.

- Static(Fixed Size)
- Dynamic

1) Static Arrays

Static array can contain fixed number of elements in array.
Example -
dim a (10) - This static array will contain only 11 elements.
If you want to increase/decrease the size of array, it will
not be possible.

2) Dynamic Arrays

In dynamic array we can change the size of array.

Dim b() - This is how we define dynamic array.
To use dynamic array we must define the size.
Redim b(5) - Array b redefined with size of 5 means it can
contain 6 elements.

22	32	1	66	8	12
0	1	2	3	4	5

Array containing 6 elements

26

Now if you want to increase the size of elements in array you can use below statment

redim b(7) - In this case array can contain 8 elements but previous elements will be erased.

0	1	2	3	4	5	6	7

To preserve the contents of the array, we can use
Redim preserve b(7)

22	32	1	66	8	12		
0	1	2	3	4	5	6	7

When we reduce the size of dynamic array , data of the array is lost.

For example if we have a array b

```
redim preserve b(8)
```

and we execute below statement

```
redim preserve b(3)
```

Then we will not be able to access the elements at the index 4 onwards.

Erasing elements in the Array

We can use erase statement to remove the data from fixed size array. Please note that memory is still occupied by the array after erasing in fixed size array.

```
'Erasing Fixed size array
Dim a(2)
a(0)=11
Erase a
```

We can use erase statement to release the memory occupied by the **dynamic array.**

```
'Erasing Dynamic Array
Dim da()
ReDim da(2)
da(0) = 12
Erase da
```

Please note that we can have multi-dimensional arrays as well.Dim twodim(5, 10)

In above array, there will be 6 rows and 11 clolumns

5. Strings in VBScript

In this chapter, you will learn how to handle strings in VBScript. You will get to know how to find the length of string, how to convert the string to uppercase and lowercase, how to find the substring, how to remove spaces from the string, how to replace the string.

String functions in vbscript

Below is the list of string functions in vb script

1. lcase
2. ucase
3. len
4. left
5. right
6. mid
7. ltrim
8. rtrim
9. trim
10. replace
11. strreverse
12. string
13. Instr
14. Instrrev
15. strcomp

In QTP, above string functions are frequently used for testing purpose. Scenarios where you will use above string functions are given below.

1. When comparing 2 strings, we need to remove spaces from the beginning and end using trim functions.
2. We also need to convert the String case to either upper case or lower case using while doing comparison.
3. Sometimes we need to get the fixed number of characters from the given string which can be done using left, mid and right functions.

We are going to have a look at each String function mentioned above.

5.1 Substring Extraction functions

Some of the commonly used string manipulation functions are given below.

- right
- mid
- left

All of the above functions are frequently used when performing any string operations in vbscript.

All of the above functions extract the part of the string / Sub string.

Right function returns the fixed number of characters from right side of the string.

Left function returns the fixed number of characters from left side of the string.

Mid function can be used to get the characters/ sub string from the left, right or middle part of the string.

Examples -

```
myString = "Sachin Plays Cricket"

Msgbox right(myString,7)
'will return the 7 characters from the
right side of myString
'Cricket
Msgbox left(myString,6)
'will return the 6 characters from the
left side of myString
'Sachin
Msgbox mid(myString,8,5)
'will return the 5 characters from the
8th position of myString
'Plays
```

Syntax -
Second parameter in left and right function tells how many characters to return from the string.
In mid functions there are 2 parameters. First parameter tells from which position of the string we have to get the characters and second parameter tells how many characters to return.

5.2 Converting Case of Strings
We can convert the string from lower case to upper case and vice versa using ucase and lcase functions in VBScript.

```
str = "We are learning strings in
VBScript"
Msgbox lcase(str)
'It will print - we are learning strings
in vbscript

Msgbox ucase(str)
'It will print - WE ARE LEARNING STRINGS IN
VBSCRIPT
```

5.3 Replacing part of the string

Replace function can be used to replace the part of the string with other string. Syntax of replace is given below.

Replace(mainString,stringToFind,replaceString[,start_Index [,Replace_count[,comparison_mode]]])

More information on the parameters is given below.

1. mainString - This is the original string
2. stringToFind - This is the string which will be searched and replaced
3. replaceString - This is the string which will replace other string in the original string
4. start_Index - Index position of the original string from where you have to search it
5. Replace_Count - How many occurrences of the string you want to replace
6. Comparison_Mode - Binary (Case Sensitive) or textual comparison (Case Insensitive). by default it is binary comparison.

Examples -

```
mainString = "Sachin plays cricket"
msgbox
replace(mainString,"Sachin","Arjun")
'Prints Arjun plays cricket.
```

5.4 Finding the length of the string

Len function is used to find the length of the string.

Example -

```
mainString = "Sachin plays cricket"
msgbox len(mainString)
'Prints 20
```

5.5 Trim functions of the string

Trim functions are used to remove the blank spaces from the beginning and ending of the string.
There are 3 functions in this category.

1. ltrim - removes blank spaces from left side of the string
2. rtrim - removes blank spaces from right side of the string
3. trim - removes blank spaces from both left and right side of the string

Example -

```
mainString = "  Sachin plays cricket  "
msgbox ltrim(mainString)
'Prints  "Sachin plays cricket  "

msgbox rtrim(mainString)

'Prints  "  Sachin plays cricket"

msgbox trim(mainString)
'Prints  "Sachin plays cricket"
```

5.6 Reverse the string in VBScript

We can use strreverse function to reverse the string in VBScript.

Example -

```
mainString = "Sachin"
msgbox strreverse(mainString)
'Prints  "nihcaS"
```

5.7 String function in VBScript

We can use string function to get the specified character n times.

Example -

```
```

```
msgbox String(5,"*")
'prints *****
```

5.8 Instr function in VBScript

We can use instr function to find the substring in given string. Searching happens from the beginning of the string.

Syntax of Instr

```
InStr([start,]string1,string2[,compare])
msgbox instr(1,"sagaar","g")
'prints 3
```

5.9 Instrrev function in VBScript

We can use instrrev function to find the substring in given string. Searching happens from the end of the string but the position of the character is counted from the beginning of the string.

Syntax of Instrrev

```
InStrRev(string1,string2[,start[,compare
]])
msgbox instrrev("sagaar","g")
'prints 3
```

5.10 Comparing 2 strings in VBScript

We can use **StrComp** function to compare two strings.

The StrComp function returns the values based upon comparison result.

1. -1 (if string1 < string2)
2. 0 (if string1 = string2)
3. 1 (if string1 > string2)
4. Null (if string1 or string2 is Null)

The syntax of the StrComp function is ->

```
StrComp (string1, string2 [,
comparison_mode])
```

The last parameter determines whether comparison is binary or textual. By default it is binary comparison (Case Sensitive).

```
msgbox strcomp("Amol","Sagar") 'prints -
1..since ascii value of A is less than
that of S
msgbox strcomp("sagar","sagar")'prints 0
msgbox strcomp("sagar","Amol") 'prints 1
```

6. Maths functions in vbscript

In this chapter, you will learn about math functions in VBScript to find the absolute value of the number, to find the square root of the numbers, to find the round of the number. You will also learn different trigonometric functions.

Below is the list of all maths functions in vb script

1. Abs
2. Atn
3. Cos
4. Exp
5. Fix
6. Int
7. Log
8. Rnd
9. Sgn
10. Sin
11. Sqr
12. Tan
13. Round

In QTP, we will need math functions in below scenarios.

1. We usually need to round the 2 numbers for comparison purpose. So we can use round function for that purpose.

2. Sometimes we need to randomly select the test data. In this case we can use Rnd function to produce some random numbers.

Let us have a look at each of these functions with examples.

```
'To find the absolute value
Msgbox Abs(-11) 'prints 11

'To round the number
Msgbox round(22.346,2)   'prints 22.35

'To find the square root of the number
Msgbox Sqr (4)  'prints 2


Msgbox Exp(2)   'e^2
```

Difference between int and fix is that - If the number is negative, int will return smallest possible integer value while fix will return largest possible integer value

For positive numbers, both int and fix work the same way.

```
Msgbox Int (-8.4)   '  returns -9
Msgbox Fix(-8.4) 'returns   -8
```

```
'Calculates natural logarithm to the
base e
Msgbox Log(10)

'gets the random number
Msgbox Rnd()

'We must use Randomize function before
Rnd to get different values

'To get the random numbers between 2
integers
max=100
min=1
Randomize
Msgbox (Int((max-min+1)*Rnd+min))
```

This functions returns the integer number -1,0 or 1 depending upon the sign of the number.

If the sign of the number is negative, -1
if the number is zero , 0
If the sign of the number is positive, 1

```
Msgbox Sgn(-11)   'prints -1
'Used for geometric calculations
Msgbox Sin(90)
Msgbox Tan(45)
Msgbox Atn(45)
Msgbox Cos(0)
```

7. Date time functions in vb script

In this chapter, you will learn about different date and time functions that can be used to find the current date and time of the system, find the future/ past date, find the difference between 2 dates.

It is very important that you know how to work with date and time in VBScript as most of the VBScript programs will have date and time involved in it.

Below is the list of all date and time functions in vb script.

1. date
2. dateadd
3. datediff
4. datepart
5. dateserial
6. datevalue
7. day
8. hour
9. minute
10. second
11. month
12. monthname
13. time
14. timeserial
15. timevalue
16. weekday

17. weekdayname

18. year

In QTP, we use date and time functions in below scenarios.

1. To find the total test execution time, we can use datediff function.

2. In banking applications, we may need to find the future and past dates. We can do it using dateadd function.

3. While creating html reports, we can use current system time and date (Now function) and print it in reports.

4. We can also verify if given date is a valid business date or not using weekday function.

We are going to have a look at each of these functions and examples in VBScript.

```
'To find current system date
msgbox " Current System date is -> " &
date
'*********************************************
********'To find the future or past date
msgbox "Tommorrow's date will be " &
dateadd("d",1,date)
```

First argument is Interval Type and it can be of below types.

yyyy - Year

m - Month

d - Day

h - Hour

n - Minute

s - Second

```
'To find the difference between 2 dates
msgbox "Day Difference between today and
tommorrow is " & datediff("yyyy","9-jan-
1986",date)
```

First argument is Interval Type and it can be of below types.

yyyy - Year

m - Month

d - Day

h - Hour

n - Minute

s - Second

```
'To find the current day like 1,2,3...28
msgbox "Current day is -> " & day(date)

'*******************************************
'To find the current hour
msgbox "current hour is -> " & hour(now)

'*******************************************
'To find the current minute
msgbox "current minute is -> " &
minute(now)

'*******************************************
```

```vbscript
'To find the current second
msgbox "current second is -> " &
second(now)
'*****************************************

'To find the current month number like
1,2....11,12
msgbox "current month is -> " &
month(now)


'*****************************************

'To find the month name like Jan,
Feb.....Dec
msgbox "current month name is -> " &
monthname(month(now))
'*****************************************

'To find the current system time
msgbox "current time is -> " & time
'*****************************************

'To find the weekday number like
1,2....7
msgbox "current weekday is -> " &
weekday(now)
'*****************************************

'To find the name of week day like
sunday, monday...saturday
msgbox "current weekday Name is -> " &
weekdayname(weekday(now))
'*****************************************

'To find the current year
msgbox "current year is ->" & year(now)
'*****************************************
```

```vbscript
'To find the parts of the given time
stamp .equivalent to day, minute,hour,
second etc
msgbox "Day part of the current
timestamp" & datepart("d",now)

'*****************************************
'To convert the string to date
msgbox "String to date -> " &
datevalue("09-jan-1986")
'*****************************************

'To convert the string to time
msgbox "String to time-> " &
TimeValue("7:15:49 PM")
'*****************************************

'To create date from numbers
msgbox dateserial(1986,01,09)
'*****************************************

'To create time from numbers
msgbox timeserial(17,01,09)
```

8. Procedures in VBScript.

In this chapter, you will learn about procedures, their uses, passing arguments to the procedures and calling them.

8.1 What is Procedure?

Sub procedures are used to perform the specific task. Sub procedures are used to increase the reusability of the code.

In QTP, we use procedures to perform some generic operation or application specific operation. We can use same procedures in multiple test cases. So this increases code reusability.

<u>Simple example of the procedure</u>

Suppose you want to find the sum of 2 numbers. Without procedures, you will write below code.

```
a = 10
b = 20
c = a+ b
Msgbox c
```

To add another 2 different numbers, you will use below code

```
a = 33

b  =  65
c  =  a+ b
Msgbox c
```

In above examples, we have to add 2 numbers. So the operation is same (Repeating) So we can write the procedure which will take 2 parameters as shown below.

```
sub sum(byref a, byref b)

    msgbox cint(a) + cint(b)

end sub
```

8.2 Calling procedures in VBScript

To call the procedures we can use below statements.

```
Call sum(10,20)
Call sum(33,65)
```

Thus we can call procedures many times in the code. This reduces the lines of code as well as maintainability of the code.

8.3 Passing arguments to the procedure

We can pass the arguments to the procedure by 2 ways.

1. Pass by reference
2. Pass by value

Pass by reference

By default, values are passed to the procedure by reference. When we pass the values by reference the changes made to the variables in the called procedure are reflected in the calling procedure.

When we pass the arguments to the procedure by reference, the address of the argument variables are passed so less memory is required.

Below Example will demonstrate how we can use Pass by reference.

```
a = 10
call findsqr(a)
msgbox a    'prints 100

sub findsqr(byref a)

   a = a*a

   msgbox a    'prints 100

end sub
```

Pass by value

When we pass the values by value, the changes made to the variables in the called procedure are not reflected in the calling procedure. More memory is required when we pass the arguments to the procedure by value as the copies of the arguments are created in the memory.

Below Example will demonstrate how we can use Pass by Value.

```
a = 10
call findsqr(a)
msgbox a    'prints 10
sub findsqr(byval a)
   a = a*a
   msgbox a    'prints 100
end sub
```

9. Functions in VBScript

In this chapter, you will learn about functions, their uses, passing arguments to the functions and calling them.You will also learn about different built-in functions in VBScript. In the end, we will see the difference between procedures and functions.

9.1 What is Function?

Functions are used to perform the specific task.Functions are used to increase the reusability of the code. Functions are similar to the procedures except one difference that functions can return value. Every function takes input in the form of arguments and produces the output which can be returned to the calling function.

In QTP, we use functions to perform some generic operation or application specific operation. We can use same function in multiple test cases. So this increases code reusability.

In keyword driven automation frameworks, we map each keyword to the function in QTP. Each function will perform specific operation in the application like login, booking and return true or false.

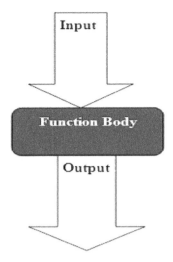

Figure 3 - Functions in VBScript

Simple example of the function

Suppose you want to find the sum of 2 numbers. Without functions, you will write below code.

```
a = 10
b = 20
c = a+ b
Msgbox c
```

To add another 2 different numbers, you will use below code

```
a = 33
b = 65
c = a+ b
Msgbox c
```

In above examples, we have to add 2 numbers. So the operation is same (Repeating) So we can write the function which will take 2 parameters as shown below.

```
function sum(byref a, byref b)

    sum = cint(a) + cint(b)

end function
```

9.2 Calling functions in VBScript

To call the functions we can use below statements.

```
c = sum(10,20)
msgbox c
c =  sum(33,65)
msgbox c
```

Thus we can call functions many times in the code. This reduces the lines of code as well as maintainability of the code.

9.3 Passing arguments to the function

We can pass the arguments to the function by 2 ways.

1. Pass by reference
2. Pass by value

Pass by reference

By default, values are passed to the function by reference. When we pass the values by reference the changes made to the variables in the called function are reflected in the calling function/procedure.

```
a = 10
c = findsqr(a)
msgbox a    'prints 100
msgbox c    'prints 100

function findsqr(byref a)

   a = a*a

   findsqr = a

end function
```

Pass by value

When we pass the values by value, the changes made to the variables in the called function are not reflected in the calling procedure or function.

```
a = 10
c = findsqr(a)
msgbox a    'prints 10
msgbox c    'prints 100

function findsqr(byval a)

   a = a*a
```

```
findsqr = a

end function
```

9.4 Important built-in functions in VBScript

1. msgbox
2. inputbox
3. eval
4. execute

msgbox function is used to show message to the user.

inputbox function is used to read the value from the user.

```
a = inputbox("Enter the number")
msgbox a 'prints 33
```

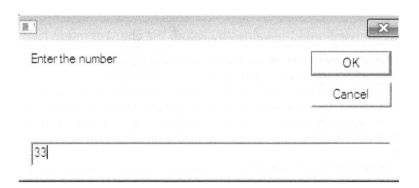

Inputbox function in vbscript

Eval and execute functions are used to execute any valid vbscript expression. Difference between 2 functions is that the operator = is handled in different ways.

Eval always uses = as a comparison operator.
Execute always uses = as a assignment operator.

```
a=20
msgbox eval("a=10")   'will print false
msgbox a

a=20
execute("a=10")
msgbox a      'will print 10
```

9.5 Difference between Functions and Procedures

Major difference between procedures and functions in vb script is that procedures can not return the value but functions can return the value.

Procedure Example –

```
Sub findsq()

   temp = InputBox("Please enter the
number", 1)
   MsgBox "square root of the num is " &
sqrt(temp)
```

```
End Sub
```

Function Example

```
a = findsq()   ' function returns the
value in variable a
msgbox a

function findsq()
  temp = InputBox("Please enter the
number", 1)
  findsq = sqrt(temp)
End function
```

10. Classes in VBScript

In this chapter, you will learn about how to define the classes in VBScript, create objects of the classes and how to define the constructors and destructors.

10.1 What is class?

Here is an example that shows how we can create a class in VBScript. Once we define the class, we can create its objects and then access its method and properties.

Using a class we can design the VBScript applications with object oriented paradigm.

10.2 Class Example in VBScript

```
'declare the class book.
Class Book

dim bn,bp
'class has 2 variable members bn and bp.

public Property Get bookname()
    ' Get bookname property gets the
book name of the object of Book
  bookname = bn
End Property

public Property Let  bookname(x)
  bn = x
    ' Let  bookname property assigns
value to the book name of the object of
Book
End Property

public Property Get price()
```

```
price = bp
End Property

public Property Let  price(x)
bp = x
End Property


function  discountedPrice()
Msgbox bp-20
'We can have functions and procedures
inside class to process memeber
variables
End function


Private Sub Class_Initialize    ' Setup
Initialize event.

MsgBox("Object of Book Class created")

End Sub

Private Sub Class_Terminate     ' Setup
Terminate event.

MsgBox("Object of Book Class destroyed")

End Sub

End Class

'*****************************************
Set b1 = new  Book
'createing the object b2 of the class
Book.

b1.bookname = "VBSCRIPT Tutorials"
```

```
b1.price = 220
'assigning value to the object b1

Msgbox b1.bookname()
'getting the value of the property
bookname.

'accessing the function in class
b1.discountedPrice()

Set b1 = nothing
```

10.3 Constructors and Destructors in VBScript

VBScript does support object oriented programming to some extent. We can create constructors and destructors in vbscript classes using class_initialize and class_terminate methods. class_initialize method acts like constructor function which gets called automatically when we create an object of the class. This is how we can create and use the classes in VBSCRIPT.

11. Regular Expressions in Vbscript

In this chapter, you will learn about how to use regular expressions in VBScript to find out the matching patterns in the given string. You will also know how to replace the matched pattern.

11.1 Definition
A regular expression is a pattern of characters(meta characters and special characters).

11.2 Applications of Regular Expressions

Regular expressions are used for -
1. Pattern Matching in Strings
2. To find the occurrences of one string/pattern in given string.
3. To replace the patterns with another string in a given text

All programming languages support the use of regular expressions.

In QTP, we can use regular expression in many places as mentioned below.

1. In Descriptive Programming
2. In Object Repository

As we know that there are 2 ways of descriptive programming.

1. Static
2. Dynamic

We can use regular expression in both the ways as mentioned below. Please note that by default all the property values are considered as regular expressions by QTP.

Regular Expressions in Static descriptive programming in QTP.

```
Browser("index:=0").page("title:=Go
ogle").Webedit("name:=q").set
"sagar salunke"
Browser("creationtime:=0").page("ti
tle:=Google").Webbutton("name:=Goog
le.*").Click
```

Please note that last statement uses regular expression to identify the button whose name starts with Google.

If your property value itself contains the special character then that should be escaped using \ character.

Example - Suppose you want to click on the link "+sagar".

Now this link contains the special character +. To click on this link, we can use below code

```
Browser("creationtime:=0").page("ti
tle:=Google").Link("innertext:=\+sa
gar").Click
```

Regular Expressions in Dynamic descriptive programming in QTP.

```
Set descriptionObject =
Description.Create()
descriptionObject("innertext").valu
e = "+sgaar"
descriptionObject("innertext").Regu
larExpression = false

'Please note that we can specify
whether the value is regular
expression or not using
RegularExpression property. By
default it is true.

Browser("index:=0").page("title:=Go
ogle").Link(descriptionObject
).click
```

This is how we can use Regular Expressions in QTP

<u>Regular expressions in Object Repository</u>

We can also use regular expressions in Object Repository.

Object repository stores the test object properties and their values. We can use regular expressions to set the values of the properties of the test object.

When we use the value as a regular expression, single test object in OR can be be used to find the multiple run time objects.

Example -

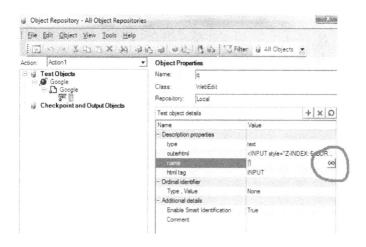

As shown in above image, we need to click on the button (circled with red) in front of the property value that you want to make as a regular expression. After you click that button, you will get below window

Then we need to enter the regular expression in the edit box and check the regular expression checkbox and click on Ok.

So now the test object will identify all the edit boxes that starts with q followed by any characters.

11.3 Examples on Regular Expressions

As I said earlier We use regular expressions to check if the given string matches the specified pattern.

For example - Consider a scenario where you have to validate that the given string should be a valid email address.

So list of valid email addresses are -
reply2sagar@gmail.com, ayx@jjjj.in etc
Some of the invalid email addresses are -
kjkjj@fdff, @dfdf.in etc

With the help of regular expression, you can easily validate the email address.

Syntax of Regular Expression in VBScript:

To write any VBScript program involving regular expressions, you will have to follow below steps.

1. Create a regular expression object (RegExp)
2. Define the pattern using RegExp object's pattern property.
3. Use test method to check whether the given string matches with the pattern specified in step 2.

```
'Create the regular expression object
Set myRegEx = New RegExp

'Specify the pattern (Regular
Expression)
myRegEx.Pattern = "[a-z0-9]+@[a-z]+\.[a-z]+"

'Specify whether the matching is to be
done with case sensitivity on or off.
myRegEx.IgnoreCase = True
```

```
'Use Test method to see if the given
string is matching with the pattern
isMatched =
myRegEx.Test("reply2sagar@gmail.com")

Variable isMatched will be true if the
string "reply2sagar@gmail.com" matches
with the given pattern
"[a-z0-9]+@[a-z]+\.[a-z]+"
```

Another example on Regular Expression.
searchString = "Sachin tendulkar is the master blaster.
Sachin lives in Mumbai and likes to play cricket."

```
searchPattern = "Sachin"
  Set reObject= New RegExp          '
Create a regular expression.

  reObject.Pattern = searchPattern   '
Set pattern.
  reObject.IgnoreCase = True          '
Set case insensitivity.
  reObject.Global = True
' Set global applicability.
  Set Matches =
reObject.Execute(searchString)    '
Execute search.

  For Each M in Matches

    Str= Str & M.Firstindex &"->" &
M.Value &  vbCRLF

  Next
```

```
Msgbox   Str

Msgbox "String after replacing -> " &
vbcrlf  &
reObject.replace(searchString,"Arjun")
```

11.4 Meta characters in regular expressions

1. \ - indicates that the next character would be a special character, a literal or a backreference
2. ^ - Input String should be matched at the beginning.
3. $ - Input String should be matched at the end.
4. * - Matches the preceding character zero or more times. It is same as {0,}.
5. + - Matches the preceding character one or more times. It is same as {1,}.
6. ? - Matches the preceding character zero or one time. It is same as {0,1}
7. {i} - Matches the previous character exactly i times.
8. {i,} - Matches the previous character at least i times and at most any time.
9. {i,j} -Matches the previous character at least i times and at the most j times.
10. . - Matches any single character except "\n".
11. (pattern) - Matches pattern and captures the match that can be used in backreferences.
12. p|q - Matches either p or q. Please note that p and q could be more complex regular expressions.
13. [pqr] - A character set. Matches any one of the character inside the brackets.
14. [^pqr] - A negative character set. Matches any character not inside the brackets.

15. [p-z] - A range of characters. Matches any character in the specified range i.e p,q,r,....x,y,z.
16. [^p-z] - A negative range characters. Matches any character not in the specified range i.e.

a,b,c...m,n,o

1. \b   - Matches the boundary of the word

2. \B   - Matches middle part of the word.

3. \d   - Matches a digit character. same as [0-9].

4. \D   - Matches a nondigit character. same as [^0-9].

5. \f , \n and \r   - Matches a form-feed character, newline and carriage character.

6. \s   - Matches any white space character including space, tab, form-feed. Equivalent to [\f\n\r\t\v].

7. \S   - Matches any non-white space character. Equivalent to [^ \f\n\r\t\v].

8. \t , \v - Matches a horizontal and vertical tab character.

9. \w   - Matches alpha numeric character including underscore. Equivalent to '[A-Za-z0-9_]'.

10. \W   - Matches any non - alpha numeric character. Equivalent to '[^A-Za-z0-9_]'.

11. \number- A reference back to captured matches.

Some examples on regular expressions:

1. To match the 10 digit mobile number -> \d{10}
2. To match email address -> \w+@\w+\.\w+

Please give your inputs, suggestions, feedback to Us about above VBScript topic. We value your thoughts.

12. Dictionary in VBScript

In this chapter, you will learn about the dictionary object and its various methods and properties that help us to add and remove the data in the dictionary. We will also see the difference between array and dictionary in VBScript.

Dictionary object is used to store the data in key-item pairs in VBScript. A Dictionary object is just like an associative array.

It stores the data in the form of key-item pairs.

Each key has some data item associated with it.

Key can be integer or string format.

Data item can be integer or string or array of variants. It may contain other dictionary itself.

In QTP, dictionary object can be used to store the data from that table.

Headers in the table will be keys for the dictionary and corresponding data in the row will be items.

12.1 Methods of Dictionary Object

1. *Add ---------> Adds new key-item pair in the dictionary object*
2. *Exists --------> returns true if the given key exists in the dictionary object*
3. *Items --------> returns the array containing all items in the dictionary object*

4. *Keys --------> returns the array containing all keys in the dictionary object*
5. *Remove -----> removes the key-item pair with given key from the dictionary object*
6. *RemoveAll --> removes all key-item pairs from the dictionary object*

12.2 Properties of Dictionary Object

1. Count-----------> returns the total number of keys in the dictionary object.
2. Item-------------> assigns or returns the item value with given key from the dictionary object.
3. Key-------------> sets the new key value for the given key
4. CompareMode -> assigns or returns the comparison mode for comparing string keys in a Dictionary object.

12.3 Example with dictionary object

Below example will illustrate how to use dictionary in VBScript.

```
'create new dictionary object
Set dictionaryObject =
CreateObject("Scripting.Dictionary")

    dictionaryObject.CompareMode = 1
```

```
    'add some key-item pairs
    dictionaryObject.Add "1", "Sagar"
    dictionaryObject.Add "2", "Amol"
    dictionaryObject.Add "3", "Ganesh"

    dictionaryObject.Key("3")  = "Bro"

    Msgbox dictionaryObject.Item("Bro")

    Msgbox dictionaryObject.Item("bro")

If  dictionaryObject.Exists("1") Then
    Msgbox "Dictionary contains key 1"
Else
    Msgbox "Dictionary does not contain
key 1"
End If

'Display keys and items  in the
dictionary
for each k in dictionaryObject.keys

    Msgbox k &"-"&dictionaryObject.item(k)

next

'Display items
for each i in dictionaryObject.items

    Msgbox  i

next

Msgbox "Total number of keys in the
dictionary are -> " &
dictionaryObject.Count
```

```
'Remove the key-item pair with key = 1
from the dictionary object
dictionaryObject.Remove("1")

'Remove all key-item pairs from the
dictionary object
dictionaryObject.RemoveAll

'Release the object
Set dictionaryObject = nothing
```

12.4 Difference between dictionary and array

Both array and dictionary are used to store the data. But we have below differences in them.

1. Everytime we use array, we have to give the dimensions of the array. But in dictionary we do not need to give the dimensions.
2. We can remove the key-item pair from the dictionary at any point of time to release the memory but in static arrays we can not do it.
3. Data in the array is stored in sequential manner while in the dictionary it is stored in key-item pair.

13. File System in VBScript

In this chapter, you will learn how to use file system object
to create, edit, delete files and folders in VBScript. You will
also know how to get the information of the drives in the
system.

Filesystemobject can be used to work with drives, folders, and
files.Filesystemobject has methods and properties that allow us
to create, delete, gain information about, and generally
manipulate drives, folders, and files.

In QTP, filesystem object is used in below scenarions.

1. Delete the report files.
2. Append the test execution log to the report file.
3. Read the data from feed files in certain applications.

Important Methods of filesystemobject in vb script

1. CopyFile
2. CopyFolder
3. CreateFolder
4. CreateTextFile
5. DeleteFile
6. DeleteFolder
7. DriveExists
8. FileExists
9. FolderExists
10. GetAbsolutePathName

11. GetBaseName
12. GetDrive
13. GetDriveName
14. GetExtensionName
15. GetFile
16. GetFileName
17. GetFolder
18. GetParentFolderName
19. GetSpecialFolder
20. GetTempName
21. MoveFile
22. MoveFolder
23. OpenTextFile

13.1 Working with files

Creating and writing to file
You can create a text file using this object.

```
Set obj=
createobject("scripting.filesystemobject
")
set f =
obj.createtextfile("g:\salunke.txt")
' create a file
f.write str   ' write some data into file
set f= nothing   ' release memory
set obj = nothing
```

Reading from the file character by character

```
Set fo= createobject("scripting.filesyst
emobject")
set stream1=
fo.OpenTextFile("c:\abc.txt",1)

msgbox stream1.AtEndOfStream

  Do While    (stream1.AtEndOfStream <>
true )
      msgbox stream1.Read(1)
  loop
      stream1.Close
  Set stream1 = nothing
```

Appending data to file

```
 set stream1=
fo.OpenTextFile("c:\abc.txt",8)
   stream1.Write("append it")

   stream1.Close
   Set stream1 = nothing
   Set fo = nothing
```

Delete a text file

```
Set fso =
CreateObject("Scripting.FileSystemObject
")
  fso.DeleteFile("c:\myfile.txt")
```

```
Set fso = Nothing
```

13.2 Working with Folders

We can create, delete and copy folders using file system object.

Example to check if the folder exists or not.

```
Set Fo =
createobject("Scripting.FilesystemObject
")
If Not Fo.FolderExists("c:\xyz")) Then
  print "Folder does not exist"
Else
  print "Folder does exist"
End If
```

Example to create the folder.

```
Set Fo =
createobject("Scripting.FilesystemObject
")
If Not Fo.FolderExists("c:\abc")) Then
    Fo.CreateFolder  ("c:\abc")
End If
```

Example to delete the folder.

```
Set fso =
CreateObject("Scripting.FileSystemObject
")
```

```
fso.DeleteFolder("c:\myfolder")
Set fso = Nothing
```

Example to copy the folder.

```
Set Fo =
createobject("Scripting.FilesystemObject")

Fo .CopyFolder
"c:\mydocuments\letters\abc",
"c:\tempfolder"

Set Fo = Nothing
```

13.3 Working with Drives

Below example will illustrate how to find the information of the drives in VBScript.

```
Dim fso, d, s

drvPath="d:"

Set fso =
CreateObject("Scripting.FileSystemObject")
    Set d =
fso.GetDrive(fso.GetDriveName(drvPath))

    msgbox " Volume name of D drive -->"
&   d.VolumeName    & vbcrlf

    msgbox  " Free Space on D drive -->"
& FormatNumber(d.FreeSpace/1024, 0)
```

14. Error Handling

In this chapter, you will learn how to use Err object to find the errors in the code and how to ignore errors in the VBScript in production environment.

VBScript provides below statements and keywords to handle errors.

1. Err object - err.description, err.number
2. on error resume next
3. on error goto 0

In QTP, we can use Err object to report errors that may occur while doing test execution. Whenever any error occurs in QTP like divide by zero, object not found, item does not exist in dropdown, Err object stores the details of the error. We can use Err object's number and description property to report the error infromation in the Test Report.

14.1 Err Object

Sample code to handle the error is given below

```
If err.number <> 0 Then

    Msgbox err.description
else
    Msgbox "there  was no error in above
statement"
```

```
end if
```

Whenever any error occurs in the script, We get the message window with detailed description of the error.

But when we are executing the scripts, we do not want this message box to appear to come as this will halt the execution of the script.

14.2 On error resume next

To prevent message box from appearing, we use below statement above the block of code.

On error resume next

----

more statements

With On error resume next in place, VBScript runs even though error exists in the code. We can capture those errors using Err object as stated earlier.

When you are debugging the scripts, you should not use On error resume next statement as it will suppress the errors and you will not be able to figure out the issue in your script.

14.3 On error goto 0

On error resume next will suppress all errors in the code. To enable error messages again in the code, you can use the statement.

On error goto 0

This statement will trigger the error message if any error occurs in the code.

15. WSH in QTP

In this chapter, you will learn WSH and various objects provided by WSH that can be used in QTP

15.1 WSH Introduction

WSH stands for Windows Script Host. WSH can be used to do below things in QTP.

1. Manipulate registry settings.
2. Access special folders like desktop.
3. Run the applications.
4. Create shortcuts to the folders.
5. Map network drives and printers.
6. Send Keys to the application.
7. Access system environment variables.

WSH provides below objects.

Object	What you can do with this object
Wscript	• Set and retrieve command line arguments • Determine the name of the script file • Determine the host file name (wscript.exe or cscript.exe) • Determine the host version information

	• Create, connect to, and disconnect from COM objects • Sink events • Stop a script's execution programmatically • Output information to the default output device (for example, a dialog box or the command line)
WshArguments	Access the entire set of command-line arguments
WshNamed	Access the set of named command-line arguments
WshUnnamed	Access the set of unnamed command-line arguments
WshNetwork	• Connect to and disconnect from network shares and network printers • Map and unmap network shares • Access information about the currently logged-on user
WshController	Create a remote script process using the Controller method **CreateScript**()
WshRemote	• Remotely administer

	computer systems on a computer network • Programmatically manipulate other programs/scripts
WshRemote Error	Access the error information available when a remote script (a WshRemote object) terminates as a result of a script error
WshShell	• Run a program locally • Manipulate the contents of the registry • Create a shortcut • Access a system folder • Manipulate environment variables (such as WINDIR, PATH, or PROMPT)
WshShortcut	Programmatically create a shortcut
WshSpecialfolders	Access any of the Windows Special Folders
WshURLShortcut	Programmatically create a shortcut to an Internet resource
WshEnvironment	Access any of the environment variables (such

	as WINDIR, PATH, or PROMPT)
WshScriptExec	Determine status and error information about a script run with Exec() Access the StdIn, StdOut, and StdErr channels

15.2 Using WSH objects in QTP

WSH objects can be used in QTP in many situations. Let us have a look at some of the examples where we can use WSH.

Launching an Application using shell object.

We can launch any application using Run Method of shell object. In below example, we have opened Internet Explorer browser.

```
Set WshShell =
CreateObject("WScript.Shell")

WshShell.Run "iexplore.exe"
```

Showing popup using shell object.

Popup method is used to show the dialog box to user.

Syntax of this method is given below.

Popup(title, timeout, text, button types/icon types)

Second parameter is timeout in seconds. If you do not respond to the pop up within timeout duration, pop up is closed automatically.

Pop up method also returns the integer number depending upon which button you click.

If you click yes, 6 is returned

If you click No, 7 is returned

If you do not respond, Nothing is returned

```
Dim WshShell, BtnCode
Set WshShell = CreateObject("WScript.Shell")


BtnCode = WshShell.Popup("did u watch
TV?", 5, "Choose:", 4 + 32)


Select Case BtnCode
    case 6    msgbox "You have not watched TV"
    case 7    msgbox "when will You watch TV?"
    case -1   msgbox "No reply"
End Select
```

Accessing Network Resources.

WshNetwork provides access to the shared resources on the network to which your computer is connected.

You create a WshNetwork object when you want to

1. Connect to network printers using AddWindowsPrinterConnection and AddPrinterConnection Method
2. Disconnect from network printers using RemovePrinterConnection
3. Set the default printer using SetDefaultPrinter Method
4. Iterate through all printers using EnumPrinterConnections
5. Map network shares using MapNetworkDrive
6. Disconnect from network shares using RemoveNetworkDrive Method
7. Iterate through network drives using EnumNetworkDrives
8. Access information about a user on the network

Example to display User and Domain information

```
Set WshNetwork = CreateObject("WScript.Network")
msgbox  "Your computer is in domain ->
" & WshNetwork.UserDomain
msgbox  "Your Computer Name is ->
" & WshNetwork.ComputerName
msgbox  "Your User Name is -
>" & WshNetwork.UserName
```

Example to Map a network drive using network object

```
Dim WshNetwork
Set WshNetwork
=CreateObject("WScript.Network")

WshNetwork.MapNetworkDrive "F:",
"\\Server\sharedfolder"
```

Example to display shared drives connections.

```
Set WshNetwork = CreateObject("WScript.Network")

Set oDrives = WshNetwork.EnumNetworkDrives

    msgbox "Your connected to below network drives"


For i = 0 to oDrives.Count - 1 Step 2
        msgbox "Drive " & oDrives.Item(i) & " =
" & oDrives.Item(i+1)


Next
```

Example to display shared printer connections.

```
Set oPrinters = WshNetwork.EnumPrinterConnections

msgbox  "You are connected to below printers"
For i = 0 to oPrinters.Count - 1 Step 2
   msgbox  "Port " & oPrinters.Item(i) & " =
" & oPrinters.Item(i+1)
   Next
```

Manipulating Environment Variables.

We can read variables from below kinds of enironment.

1. System
2. User
3. Process
4. Volatile

Below example will read all System Environment variables. To read User environment variables, just replacse System by User.

```
Set wshShell = CreateObject(
"WScript.Shell" )
Set wshUserEnv =
wshShell.Environment( "System" )
For Each strItem In wshUserEnv
      WScript.Echo strItem
Next
```

```
Set wshUserEnv = Nothing
Set wshShell   = Nothing
```

We can also add/edit/remove environment variables.

```
Set wshShell = CreateObject(
"WScript.Shell" )

Set wshSystemEnv =
wshShell.Environment( "SYSTEM" )
' Display the current value
WScript.Echo "MyVar=" &
wshSystemEnv( "MyVar" )
```

```
' Set the environment variable
wshSystemEnv( "MyVar" ) = "My
Variable Value"

' Display the result
WScript.Echo "MyVar=" &
wshSystemEnv( "MyVar" )
' Delete the environment variable
wshSystemEnv.Remove( "MyVar" )
' Display the result once more
WScript.Echo "MyVar=" &
wshSystemEnv( "MyVar" )
Set wshSystemEnv = Nothing
Set wshShell     = Nothing
```

<u>Manipulating Registry Keys.</u>

Shell object provides methods to read and write registry keys.You must be very careful while editing registry key as it may crash your system.

Here is the sample code to read registry key.

```
'Create a shell object

Set WshShell =
CreateObject("WScript.Shell")
'Read the value of key from the
registry
```

```
bvalue =
WshShell.RegRead(varpathofkey)
' in above function we have to pass
the path of key in registery.
' e.g. HKCU\Software\ie\settings
msgbox bvalue
```

16. WMI in QTP

In this chapter, you will learn WMI and how it can be used in QTP.

16.1 WMI Introduction

WMI stands for windows management instrumentation. It is a management technology for Windows operating system.

WMI complies with the standards set by the Distributed Management Task Force (DMTF). The DMTF is an industry organization that works with key technology vendors, including Microsoft, as well as affiliated standards groups to define interoperable management solutions.

We can use WMI to get system information as mentioned below.

1. To view, edit settings of desktop and server systems.
2. To view, edit settings of applications, networks.
3. To manage resources like disk drives, event logs, files, folders, file systems, networking components, operating system settings, performance data, printers, processes, registry settings, security, services, shares, users, and groups (using WMI class) in the enterprise in a consistent way.

So in short, we can manage any resource (hardware as well as software) in windows based systems.
WMI has 3 layers as mentioned below.

1. Managed resources
2. WMI infrastructure
3. Consumers

15.2 WMI examples in QTP

WMI has many WIN32 classes which provide an easy way to get information about resources of the system.

Here is the list of some of the classes.

1. Win32_Process
2. Win32_Environment
3. Win32_Desktop
4. Win32_Timezone
5. Win32_ComputerSystem
6. Win32_OperatingSystem
7. Win32_Registry
8. Win32_ScheduledJob
9. Win32_LocalTime

Now let us have a look at some of the examples.

1. Closing the process by name using **Win32_Process Class**

While testing the applications with automation, we need to close existing applications and then start new one to avoid a clash.

Below example demonstrates how we can close all processes with given name.

Suppose if you want to close all excel processes, then you can use below code.

```
Call closeProcessByName("excel.exe")
```

Suppose if you want to close all internet explorer browser processes, then you can use below code.

```
Call closeProcessByName("iexplore.exe")
```

In similar way you can close any process given that you know the name of process

```
Sub closeProcessByName(byval
process_name)

    sComp = "."
    'Get the WMI object
    Set WMI =
GetObject("winmgmts:\\" &  sComp &
"\root\cimv2")
    'Get collection of processes
with process_name like excel.exe,
iexplore.exe
  Set allp = WMI.ExecQuery("Select *
from Win32_Process Where Name = '"
& process_name & "'")
        'terminate each process
```

```
   For Each p  in allp
      p.Terminate()
   Next

End Sub
```

2. Reading Environment values using **Win32_Environment Class.**

```
Set objWMIService = GetObject(
"winmgmts://./root/CIMV2" )
strQuery = "SELECT * FROM
Win32_Environment WHERE
Name='TEMP'"

Set colItems =
objWMIService.ExecQuery( strQuery,
"WQL", 48 )

For Each objItem In colItems
     WScript.Echo "Caption
: " &  objItem.Caption
     WScript.Echo "Description
: " &  objItem.Description
     WScript.Echo "Name
: " &  objItem.Name
     WScript.Echo "Status
: " &  objItem.Status
     WScript.Echo "SystemVariable
: " &  objItem.SystemVariable
```

```
      WScript.Echo "UserName
: " &  objItem.UserName
      WScript.Echo "VariableValue
: " &  objItem.VariableValue
Next

Set colItems     = Nothing
Set objWMIService = Nothing
```

www.ingramcontent.com/pod-product-compliance
Lightning Source LLC
Chambersburg PA
CBHW060950050326
40689CB00012B/2624